SOUL BURGERS

SECOND EDITION

CHRISTINA REIHILL

© 2010 Christina Reihill/Soul Burgers

All rights reserved. No part of this publication may be
reproduced in any form or by any means—graphic, electronic
or mechanical, including photocopying, recording, taping or
information storage and retrieval systems—without the prior
written permission of the authors.

978-1-908024-13-8

A cip catalogue for this book is available from the
National Library.

Drawings by Zita Reihill.

Cover and interior design by Joey Teehan.

To my parents

ACKNOWLEDGEMENTS

There are so many to thank for this 15-year journey. I feel indebted beyond words to those mentioned in the first edition but particular thanks for this edition goes to: Maura Russell, Barbara Fitzgerarld, Joan O'Donovan, John McKale, Marianne Gunne O'Connor, Eoin O Chionnaith, Clodagh Finn, Nick Kereszi, Mary McGrath, Deryn Mackay and all at Khan, Grace Smith, Anne Aslett, Dr. Brigid O'Connell, Carrie Crowley, Marian Keyes, Comhaltas Ceoltóirí Éireann, and Charlotte Bradley. An enormous thank you to the team at the Sunday Independent – particularly Anne Harris and Madeleine Keane.

My deepest gratitude goes to my family, particularly my father John Reihill who, from the moment I went into treatment for drug and alcohol addiction, stayed by my side in all weathers. Mark Inglefield, who taught me that divorce is as challenging and rewarding a spiritual container as marriage. Seamus and Betty Collins, my cousins, Dr. Ruth Collins and Ailbhe Harrington. My siblings Zita, Johnny, Mark, Raymond and Karen have also shared this road, reminding me that difference makes for rich relationships and that there are many ways through. A special thanks to Zita who provided the lovely drawings for the text.

"In the depth of winter I finally learned that there was in me an invincible summer."

ALBERT CAMUS

The first poem in my recovery story told in verse was inspired by a drunk woman sitting in a restaurant who reminded me of me.

I was there with a friend, a doctor who'd taken me under his wing since I'd stopped drinking and he, like me, was trying to abstain from his drug of choice, morphine.

We were about to order our food when I saw this woman a few tables away. I was transfixed.

I couldn't take my eyes off her. She was wearing a red hat and was pouring a large glass of red wine into her emaciated frame. She looked like a wooden doll.

As soon as I returned home, I grabbed a pen and paper and the opening poem of this book, Living Dead, landed on the page.

I seized other potent moments like that one and wrote another poem... then another, until one day I had nearly 150 poems, each one describing a section of the rope that had pulled me from breakdown to breakthrough.

Later, when I trained as a psychotherapist and had heard many stories like mine, telling of one rock bottom or another, whether it was a broken marriage or loss of identity, I discovered that there is a universal spiritual map to wholeness, which academics, philosophers, psychologists and gurus had recognized long before me.

But excited that I'd found a new map explaining something so hard to grasp, I embarked on a mission to produce a simple guide for these travellers of the soul.

I spent years studying and researching various blueprints on the subject till I was led to Dante's 14th-century building block to wholeness, The Divine Comedy. This extraordinary text was the closest blueprint to what I'd written – it was a very sophisticated version of the lyrical narrative I'd produced.

So I traced his vivid and visceral theme of love and mapped 64 of my poems on to his hazardous and glorious climb to wholeness and – like his unique narrative style – my climb is described in the present tense so the reader takes the journey alongside the poet of my story.

My poems stand alone as snapshots of a journey to wholeness but, as a rolling narrative, this is my contemporary Everyman story to personal freedom.

And so to my rapper's version of The Divine Comedy – an ordinary story telling of an extraordinary journey.

In 2010, I staged a theatre production of Soul Burgers with wonderful talents including a professional actress and a troupe of Irish musicians to communicate the rich quality of its depth and span of experience.

Following its success, I explored other 'theatrical' ideas to communicate a three-dimensional concept of poetry which included a Pop-Up Poetry shop and poetry recitals with Uillean pipes/lower flute at organic food markets in Dublin.

The concept of The Poet and The Piper, a touring duet, found its origins here.

This is the book of poems that accompanied "Listen", the theatre production, but to provide some context for readers, I'm outlining my story of addiction.

The year was 1995 and after years of living like that lady in the restaurant, too drunk to care any more and lost in a world I didn't understand without alcohol or drugs in my system, I found myself sitting with a therapist and talking about my wish to end it all.

At the time, I was 33, separated and about to lose yet another job as a journalist on a glossy magazine.

"I want to die," I told the therapist, who'd once worked with Mother Teresa and was my first guide on this 15-year journey.

I hadn't planned my end in any concrete way but as I sat in her converted stable that afternoon, I started to plot my final hour; vodka with Valium always appealed.

But something pulled me back from my dark thoughts, maybe it was the heavy silence in the room or the steely presence of this lady who was to become my guide for the next seven years.

"You have a duty to live your life," she said breaking the prickly silence between us.

This was not what I wanted to hear but as a fire of defiance shot up inside me (I wanted to shout, "Fuck you!") I knew my knee-jerk reaction rankled with what was true.

It was a stark, startling moment, one of many that defined our weekly meetings and changed the course of my life.

Weeks or maybe it was months later, when my depression lifted and I began to trust this quietly spoken lady (her name was Maura), I parked my morbid thoughts and surrendered to her teachings.

Along the way, I attended 12-step meetings, completed a four-year Diploma in psychotherapy, practiced as a psychotherapist and studied with many other mentors who taught me what it means to be human.

But back to the beginning of my journey with Maura and the moment that inspired this story.

It was the year Japan had suffered an enormous earthquake; Bill and Hillary Clinton visited Ireland; the ban on selling Playboy in newsagents had been lifted and OJ Simpson won his murder trial, but none of that mattered to me.

That year, the only earthquake I was aware of was happening inside me.

For almost a year, I talked obsessively about a sense of missing that had haunted me all my life and one which I used alcohol and drugs to fill and forget, until they stopped working.

Week after week, Maura indulged my despair and at the same time, week after week, she asked me what I wanted from our sessions. A year later, or maybe it was more, when I felt ready to dream again, I answered her question.

"I want to know the meaning of love. I want to feel whole and live without fear. I want to know passion and the fires of longing that can take me above and beyond myself. I want personal freedom," I told her more clumsily than I've written it here.

And so began our alliance for my Heart Manifesto which involved trawling through a past buried in confusion, denial and much distorted thinking.

The result is this, Soul Burgers, a ten-year diary in verse describing the rugged landscapes of illusion and desire – my soul's journey to discover the meaning of love as I learned the tough lessons on what it's not.

For example, I learnt that romance has little or nothing to do with love and much to with addiction.

Like Dante's 700-verse climb, my back-pack version telling of the peaks, valleys and vast lands of waiting in between, is told in three chapters, The Sleep, The Wake and The Dawn.

More elaborately, Soul Burgers tells of an evolving consciousness. It's a Western map to the Buddhist's teachings to freedom. It's one person's climb from the first mind to the fourth mind of awareness.

This is my version of Schiller's road to "the universal kiss" (the mind that lives in faith and trust, The Shaddha) – a song to the dark night of the soul, urging the True-Self to be born.

This travelogue is what mythologist Joseph Campbell termed the Hero's Journey, what psychologist Carl Jung referred to as the reach for "God consciousness" and what the Hindus call, Satyan, Shivam and Sunderam: the flower of truth, good and beauty.

And like all these spiritual quests, mine begins at an end with a sense of brutal rejection.

Because in the end, I didn't give up alcohol – alcohol gave up on me. If it still gave me the buzz and self-confidence it once did, I'd be drinking now.

Somewhere along the way what was once a shortcut to feeling good became a poison. Alcohol began to consume me. It dominated every thought and deed of my day: When could I start drinking? What could I drink? What amount, with whom, with what amount of cocaine?

I knew what I was doing was corroding the core of me but I was addicted. I was miserable, often suicidal, but however many suicide notes I wrote, I lacked whatever it takes to step over that final line and always woke to the same the following day.

I remember the moment I decided that enough was enough. It was an autumn evening in London and a former beloved was coming into town and invited me out for dinner.

I began coaching myself, trying to arrange my thoughts to make going out drinking with this man a perfectly normal, non-destructive exercise.

At the time, I was trying to convince myself I wasn't an alcoholic – I planned to change my drink (from spirits to wine), my friends (get rid of the heavy alcoholics around me) and my job (park journalism for something less demanding), but I had absolutely no intention of getting rid of the only thing that was ruining me.

Apart from that, I didn't want to end the night in the usual way with this person. I loved him and always enjoyed our evenings together, but it always went too far and left me feeling humiliated and used.

Delighted with my self-coaching session, I donned an outfit of velvet and lace and took a last look in the mirror. "You look great," I told myself, and then, in my sternest voice, I added: "If you break this promise to yourself, you're going to have to admit you're an alcoholic."

But I often said that to frighten myself before a night out, so there was nothing new in that. The evening was a complete disaster.

I met my friend and had dinner. When I say we had dinner, I didn't eat – I had given up eating and drinking at the same time. We drank as we always did, but there was something wrong.

The alcohol was betraying me. It wasn't getting me to where it was meant to get me. I was meant to be reaching some form of oblivion, but I was in limbo. No man's land. I wasn't drunk and I certainly wasn't sober. I just left the bar, poured myself into a taxi and went home. Alone.

Within minutes of arriving back at the flat, I was on my hands and knees begging my dead grandmother for help. I'd fallen in various states of despair before, but something shifted in my soul that night.

The next morning, I woke up and grabbed the phone beside my bed and pleaded with a friend to take me to my first AA meeting. I rattled from head to toe for the hour in a state of horror and relief, but hearing nothing. A few weeks later, I bought a one-way ticket home to Ireland with a broken marriage, a broken career and too many fragmented memories.

My relationship with alcohol was difficult from the start, but my attraction to its romance in a glass, 15 years from my last drink, can be as vivid and magnetic today, as it was when I had my first drink after a party at home, at the age of nine.

Some days I never think of a drink or a drug (I was addicted to cocaine by the time I was 30), but other times I can find myself gripped with an animal desire for its promise of oblivion.

Many I know in recovery from all sorts of addictions, be they alcohol, sex, gambling or worry, claim they don't get compulsions like mine, but from the time I made a first attempt to deal with my addictive personality, I've been besieged by compulsions of one kind or another.

An intense four-year training in psychotherapy has taught me to discipline these urges, but I have to work hard to manage their raw reminders that just one glass of my past could throw away a hard-won sobriety.

One of six children, and twin to a boy, I was always rebellious. Perhaps it's due to my mother's early death, when she was 36 and I was just 10, but I have never embraced the traditional notion of happy-ever-after. I knew life was more complicated than that.

I wanted to know what happened to my mother and why death seemed to release a gas of silence – no one wanted to talk about that.

I was lost and looking for guidance and found the road for me at the age of 16 before a school disco in Bray.

To this day, the memory of that first glass of beer still brings warm feelings to my heart. As soon as I swallowed that bottle of Harp, all the internal conflicts bouncing like tennis balls inside my mind just disappeared.

One minute I was nervous and feeling self-conscious as thoughts of going to my first school disco rattled through my body, but the next, after I kissed that blonde in a glass, I was Lucy in the sky with diamonds, cruising across the dance floor with "I'm edible" written across my lips.

And for the next 15 years, I chased that 'you're gorgeous' feeling, however hideous the consequences.

As a journalist in London in the 1980s, I lived a charmed life of late-night boozing in the Groucho Club or Green Street, a favourite Boho house in the West End. But even when that was closing at 3am or 4am, the night could still be young for me.

Depending on whom I met or whether there was cocaine to fuel a few more hours of intense but impersonal contact, I could stumble home alone or find some place to lay my crumpled hat.

There was much innocent fun before those nights lost their dignity for me. In my early days at 'Vogue' magazine, all that glittered was gold. As a 'Voguette' drenched in pearls and a new set of political convictions I started living with Henry, a beautiful boy who was educated at Eton and had much to show me.

In that hub of love, I discovered a taste for the exotic and the new as we danced a life of gay abandon, experimenting with drugs, each other and all that felt forbidden and sweet. Boys danced and kissed with boys, girls danced and kissed with girls in a paradise of silver baubles and endless romance.

Bea Miller was the editor of British 'Vogue' in those days. Lunches poured into dinners and I drove, drunk, up and down the country in my job. I'd arrive late at my desk, recovering from hangovers, strange bruises and wince-inducing memories of the night before.

I'd leave the house swearing not to drink; 10 hours later, I'd be drunk, lying to myself and anyone else who'd listen.

The sudden death of my step-brother Hugo in the early 1990s triggered a descent into a new hell. Every road ahead felt like a David Cronenberg film – out of the crash of last night's drinking and drugging, all I could see was another drive through the nightmare.

Every time I looked behind, all I could see was a pile of devastation. No one driving past seemed to want to stop for me, or maybe I didn't want them to just yet. Healthy people with purpose in their lives were not interested in me and, as difficult as it is to admit now, I held nothing but contempt for them. I was determined to stay asleep.

Much of my drinking and drugging was with other lost characters. I wasn't a secret drinker, as many women with a drinking problem can be. I used to convince myself that I wasn't alcoholic, and it was very important to me to be in company, whatever kind of company it might be.

In my mind, I was sorely misunderstood and deserved unique attention. I worked on other big glossies after 'Vogue' but found myself lost in the advertising departments. I was of course drinking and drugging at the time and, amazingly, selling space thanks to long boozy lunches with hard-boiled media buyers, who ended up admitting that they hated their jobs after I shredded their facades and told them that they were just as lost and messed up as me. The memory of my behaviour makes me shudder as I write.

But one of my publishers at the time was great fun and I spent many long nights partying with her and her heavy-metal guitarist boyfriend, but in the end, she let me go, saying she was sorry but it was her or me (the sales figures were down and I had to take the fall).

Following another spell off the booze and drugs, I found myself at a party where someone asked me if I'd like to join a small Irish team launching 'The Digger', a satirical magazine that was going to compete with 'Private Eye'.

I liked the idea of that – a small Irish publication taking on the might of an English institution, albeit an irreverent one, and it was there I met Mark, my husband-to-be.

He was beautiful-looking and great fun, and a year later, after he'd read some of my writing material, he encouraged me to do a journalism course and follow my dreams of being a writer and to this day, I'm forever indebted to him for that.

We hosted many dinner parties in our home in Notting Hill Gate. Table after table of friends joined us for hours of entertainment.

At that time, I think I may have seen myself as Vita Sackville-West but, as I look back now, I was a sad drunk with bad skin and a boring story nobody wanted to hear.

During this period of my descent into alcoholism, strangers became my intimates, while friends unable to deal with my drinking became strangers to me.

Everyone has limits and I tested them all, until the only people who accepted me were the voices at the end of the line of a call to the Samaritans or Alcoholic Anonymous.

By now, my career as a magazine journalist was almost over. I moved into freelance newspaper work until the alcohol and drugs worked me. When I could no longer produce copy without my hands shaking, I decided on another career path, and so to my brief but colourful career as a delicatessen girl.

My head was fried trying to give up the booze and just staying with the coke. This recipe for living wasn't working anywhere. If you came into the shop and asked for bread, you'd get a cup of coffee. And if you wanted some cheese, I stood in front of the beautiful counter full of cheese and told you we didn't have any.

In the end, I was living on three hours' sleep, working as a post girl dropping leaflets in strange suburbs of London.

Indeed, 10 sackings later, more bounced cheques, unpaid bills, drunk-driving stops and strangers at the bar, I was yet to hit my rock bottom.

And even when I returned home to Dublin, there was another year of flopping in bars and bumping into very chilly parts of myself before I threw in my last glass of wine.

And the lady in the restaurant, who inspired the opening poem Living Dead in the lyrical narrative that follows, is a helpful reminder to keeping me sober and doing my best to listen to "the still small voice" of my intuition and allow its wisdom and belief in a world beyond my understanding to guide my choices today.

"You need chaos in your soul to find the dancing star," said Nietzsche and so to the journey through the forest and the clearing I now call my life.

Welcome to my song to Love.

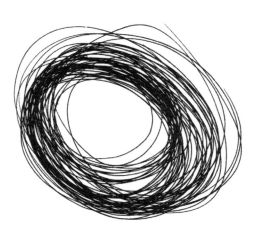

The Sleep

A red cloche hat
Red lipstick
Red nails
Eyes pooled in sadness
I sat living a lie

And I knew it
Words dribbling from my mouth
A cigarette pinched between "V" fingers
A pint glass by my side
I lied and lied and lied

"I don't remember," I said
Blowing a bubble from this mouth
Perched on the chair
Stone faced, hollowed heart
Pleading, death take me on a cart

A wooden doll
Talking
Drinking
Smoking
Smiling but not joking

Splintered, sodden, soaking
Drinking, talking, smoking
A moment hoping
A flicker in those puddled eyes
Forgetting my life's a pack of lies

Food strayed on my plate
No more drinking, no more talking
Numbed at last
Veiled future, curtained past
No more lies needing masks

My partner set to leave
I didn't want to stay
I didn't want to leave
Who cares, I thought
Not me

Who are you
Midnight caller
Shadow of my dreams
Grand masks of lost eternity

What do you plead
Dancing in your feint
Mouthing "quelle horreur"
Leaning me to wake

Are you my past
Are you my present
Are you my path enfold

Hush
I hear you now
Tame sail of all forgotten

You are my past
You are present
You are my story told

I bit my lip
And walked in there
I saw your faces
And you did stare
You searched my eyes for truth and dare
Defiant, I glared back
Blocking, blocking all out there

You looked again
Dismissing my will
I shifted uneasily
As time stood still
You spoke directly I ducked and dived
You needled away
I ran and ran and ran to hide

You pinned me with another gaze
I erupted in fantastic rage
Again you calmly sat right there
Never moving, moving an inch in the chair
I cursed your intrusion spun meaningless words
But still you sat patient
Silently wilful, wilful like hungry birds

Feelings, feelings you begged me honour
Theory upon theory, I robbed, tore and borrowed
"Forget the theory!" you mouthed aloud
"It's enough for me!" I stamped, thumped and lied
Feelings, feelings you demanded again
"Fuck off!" I screamed inside my head
Feelings, feelings burned inside

There was nowhere to run, nowhere to hide
And then as though a plug untied
Draining ache, I'd never cried
"I'm hurt," I uttered like a helpless child
"We're listening," you said, as my denial died

And so in choice, I lane my life
Signed in illusion
Bound in body
Tugged to flight
Birthed to being

When I went out walking last night
I could hear the breeze whisper, I could feel its lips bite,
When I stared out over the still shone sea,
I could hear its stillness shuffle, I could feel it hug me

I'm standing raw naked,
I've been stripped bare,
The sweet scent of your breath chokes me,
Your slippered feet scare

The past is so distant
The future, far away
I'm trapped in the now
And it frightens me today

Frozen in the present
Exposed alone
At times, I dearly wish
My heart would turn to stone

Feelings feelings scorch my insides
If only I could release them,
Like wide open tides

But it's not safe
It never was
I'm pleading faith
In watchful night stars…

A safe door closed
A rifle shot
Now that you're gone
I feel forgot

A thundering silence
A windless place
I seek your reach
But there's no chase

Cruising time
Cruising space
Cruising life's sea
Keeping pace

Time to think
Time to feel
Time to hug
The whole of me

No longer blown
No longer torn
No longer yearning
I'd never been born

A moment opened
A moment given
A moment to swim
Nakedly forgiven

Is there a voice swallowing a voice
Is there a whisper pouring more
Is there an echo swilling that sound
Hush…
Listen…
I hear a call…

Is a veil filming that face
Is a mask sealing more
Is an ache bubbling that smile
Hush…
Listen…
I hear a call…

Is a mirror smearing a question
Is a thought tricking more
Is a curious child in there
Hush…
Listen…
I hear a call…

Is hope minding defeat
Is hurt holding more
Is a caring ear in there
Hush…
Listen…
I hear a call…

Grief
Weightless time
Whispered hope
Longing for
Joys of dope

Kill the pain
Numb the brain
Sink the feeling
Fuck the healing

Down the hatch
My loveless match
Booze and drugs
Time out, snatch

A death in darkness
A death in light
Who gives a shit
I own my life!

I handed you my patchwork quilt
I watched you smile
I watched you tilt

You closed your eyes and cradled its weight
I heard you sigh
I heard you state:

"I like the density, I like the shape
But an alternative stitch
Will enhance its make"

"Its width and length could blanket a bed
Tuck it here
For a sofa instead"

"I like the fabric, I like the tones
But a different thread
Would strengthen its bones"

I held the spread of your needled advice
The texture was rough
But the wrapping was nice

Sometimes this road seems pitched in black
Mannequins shadow the front
Mannequins shadow the back
A light peeps ahead but breathes no heat;
The velvet vapours of Venus soul
The cotton caress of human being
I dive inside to bury my face from the cold
It slaps back a mirror
No feather mould
All liquid love seizes to stone
I thaw its sake
I'm less alone…

As misted rain on distant shores
As lions sleep in silent roars
As flowers scent to tickle space
Therein the melt of a frozen place

I felt your glow inside of me
Slip shone the light of Trinity
Farewell my exile on arid ground
In float of you I was found

In the temperate tear of Eve's unveil
In the watery chime of wistful wait
In the luscious lull of care's cool call
In the winsome wink of sweet soft vision

In the fuzzy vapour of fainting rain
In the tailing ache of a squint's tall-turn
In the lake of careless waves gone by
In the pulled pocket of an empty echo

In the sacrificial spray of a peacock's tail
In the scented pour of a petal's peep
In the ballooning prayer of a waltzing dream
In the bathing brush of day's broad blanket…

Sometimes there seems no point.

No point to live, no point to die
No point to laugh, no point to cry

No point to aim, no point to achieve
No point to go, no point to leave

No point to give, no point to take
No point to learn from any mistake

No point to words, no point to speech
No point to love or seek its reach

And so the void that steals to fall
The keeper of what seems
A hollow cast in prison seal
A cage in frozen dreams

No light to lift
No earth to heel
All round the route to empty
What locks this cell in terror melt
What yells this tell in me!

A pocket of dark!
A roll in coal!
Afloat in limbo loss!
The knowing of this punctured love
Nails me upon a cross

I am alone!
I am without!
I am a child betrayed!
The birthing of my soul betrothed
Slayed me 'til I obeyed!

That's where I went
That's what I learnt
My betrayal of me!
Fallen from a ground of sure
I lost the will to be

Was that my tomb of funeral
Was that my death in wake
Was that my fall from heaven's gate
Was that my suffering sake

And this three days from Easter
I am alive once more
What calls me to that open door
What walks me tall at all...

In the silence of silence
Words drag to drift of cotton clouds
Thoughts tumble to the splash of spent rain
Dreams hide in the presence of presence
And I too weary to move, stay…

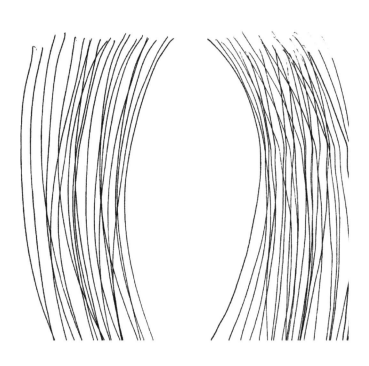

The Wake

Where am I now, I do not know
I wander lost in winter snow
I hold your name, I see your face
I open my mouth but there's no chase…

I've forgotten the language of stray-soul lives
I've bolted the Gulag of husbands and wives
I've voyaged past the post of masks
I greet the sculptures of hollow casts

I shadow the child I barely was
I gape in wonder at blinking stars
Muffled from the noise around
I breathe a sea in underground

I hear Yeti feet pound out there
I hear coughing children crying for air
I hear aching bodies frozen in voices
I hear frozen voices chilled in choices

Where has my shipwreck shored from storm?
Who is this snow-blind child I've borne?
On new-found land we brave our beginning
Scrunching footprints in fear and sinning…

Alive in thought in silent night
I plead a truth is near in sight
It taunts me in my working day
It gnaws my insides in every way

It scars my face of masquerade
It haunts my dreams of idle play
In a shop or on the street
It threatens every being I meet

I don't know what it wants to hear
I don't know why it wants my tears
"But it's not safe," I assure it that
"That's a lie!" it lashes back

Watchful, it assumes the voice of reason
Waiting, it assumes the dress of season
Wallowing, it keeps its head down low
Then furiously vengeful, it vomits its load

An artless remark, a broken plate
A weather report, any blameless bait
Fielding war zones of indiscretion
It shoots its bile in every direction

What's going on inside of me!
I've lost all sense of gravity
It has me dancing in a panic
Naked fear is running frantic

Majesty nature is unconsoling
I'm a bully, I'm controlling!
I need to sleep, I need to wake
Everything I do is a hideous mistake

I want to run, I want to hide
I want my mother by my side
But none of these are in my reach
What is the lesson, I'm ready to teach!

Of course accept, of course let go
Mother the screaming child, I know!
Perhaps that truth is there to see
But that notion of love is lost in me

So I'm hurtling down that cul-de-sac
Where seductive history is kissing my back
Whispering lies of promised love
I punish my child for my fuck up…

It peeps
Seeps
Creeps
Like a leak under the door

It's silent
Sleepless
Slavishly slow
Deaf to the word "no"

I swish
Sweep it to one side
It curls back
Like a wide open tide

I allow it in
It reaches up
Pleads ears with its eyes
Safe, sadness cries…

If I could sit and write a letter
I'd write forever to you
Wishes and wishes would fill the page
Until I fished you through...

If I could lift a phone and talk
I'd call you day and night
Words and words would fill the hours
Until I sung you back...

If I could fly or drive or climb
Or sit and meditate
I'd hold my breath on a moutain top
To ease your thieving ache...

All books and else and time deny
The loss that has no name
Because my heart peels back its want
Your "gone" is raw today...

A burn so red it scars in blue
A longing so deep, it's new
Your voice, your hand, your scented sound
My world still waits for you...

In the dance of dust darkness
When the restlessness of sleep wakes
Images of distant known voices
Inculcate the voices of foreign beings
And here the orchestra of my swan song sings

As thoughts melt under the sun of sure light
As the shadows of this waltz speaks
Louder than the skies of thunder
Quieter than the breath of beings tune
Unfleshed, I float in the womb of my who

In struggle to land my truth of truth
I splash and thrash in the drum of death's hum
Fearful in the dive of what I'm looking for
My treasure, my precious pearl of IS
Now, I surface the this of this

The fact
The truth buried in the lie
The yolk inside the egg
The pupil of the eye

You were not there
You didn't want to be
You swam in your pain
I drowned outside

You wept inside
You cried your ache
You chose to be alone
I didn't

You could yell out
You could seek help
You could have lied
I couldn't

You had the language
You had the words
You had the choice
I didn't

You blinded my eyes
You deafened my ears
You cut my throat
I bled for years

You denied your life
You denied mine
You offered me life
I hate you

The ache of no name
The ache of standing still
The ache of lost to fall
The ache of severed limb

The ache of no console
The ache of infinite spill
The ache of pulled and pour
The ache of swallowed sin

The ache of open heart
The ache of gathered gone
The ache of red in raw
 The ache of shared song

The ache of wake
The ache of long
The ache of faith
The ache of On

And then the music stopped
But the band inside my head played on
Wishing and wanting, wishing and wanting
Desire fired up its anthem song

Broken notes, rhythm wrong
The band inside my head played on
A different tune, a different song
Desire, desire, scored on and on…

Clash, clang, thud, throng
Choked, I hear a tribal song
Building castles in the sky
Desire drowns out my lover's cry

No notes, no song
Stranded on an empty long
I've lost my way, I've strayed too far
Desire you rape my heart's belong!

And now the letting go
Worn thoughts, worn dreams, worn ways
As winter wraps another year
I leave those hope-filled days

The love that was, the love that is
The love that seeks new names
Where are the lamps of midnight lambing
Where are the grasses grazed

Wet days, long nights, the drag of plod and on
Wet days, long nights, the pull of loss and gone
Another year, another song, another layer of feeling
Bring on the death, bring on the birth, bring on
the sun of healing

Submerged within the core of me
A cloud of heat froths furiously
It has no words
It has no sound
What bubbles beneath my underground!

The face of a child traces its smoky veneer
Is this a host of boiling tears?
It has no words
It has no sound
As I smother its voice with reason out loud

"There's nothing there!" feeds flapping ears
My mantra message for years and years
Damning words
Damning sound
Starving myself and sniffing hounds

Is this the moment to open the door?
Permit the mound of moisture to pour
Without words
Without sound
A thunder of wonder is willing to land…

In tidal churns of wish-spun turns
She bathed her dreams of you
In summer-sprayed hopes of rainbow slopes
She splashed her sprinkle of you
In leafy flops of carefree drops
She cradled her swathe of you
In scented shores of pastel pours
She cleansed her pure of you

In misty fogs of drifting logs
She paddled her tow of you
In Winter winds of wiping spins
She scaled her hail of you
In convent caves of failing trails
She knelt her low of you
In hollow halls of hospital floors
She stole her steal of you

In slipping scores of empty shores
She swam her reach of you
In Autumn weaves of faded leaves
She wrapped her wait of you
In darkened nights of dimming lights
She prayed her faith in you
In silent skies of frozen cries
She thawed her freeze in you
In broken days of dozing daze
She woke her sleep of you

In the pause of lost illusion
In the forest of dancing dreams
In the breath of whistled whisper
I feel the wait, the want, the watch of will's go

In the hollow of a second
In the weight of full empty
In the flight of fused flutter
I feel the urge, the push, the yawn of sleep's slow

In the hold of waking thunder
In the break of broken dam
In the splash of landed arrival
I feel the squeeze, the pull, the ache of birth's know

If I walk on your pathway
Would you see me at all
If I wave at your gate
Would you know that I called

If I knock on your door
Would you hear me inside
If I fall to the ground
Would you meet me in kind

If I say that I'm hungry
Would you invite me in
If I turn on my heel
Would you judge me in sin

If I state that I'm weary
Would you offer me a bed
If I wished to be alone
Would you accept that instead

If you receive me in this
And not turn me away
I'd cherish your home
And remember my stay…

As autumn licks long summer nights
As darkness thirsts the drench of lights
As snowflakes ache the ease of fall
I seek your hold to stay…

As teardrops stream forgotten paths
As faces front a thousand masks
As lips swan seas to steal a kiss
I seek your hold to stay…

As roses flop in velvet tongues
As sweet scent slips away
As fear kneels faith to cross the crowd
I seek your hold to stay…

In the nearness of end
As the tide of night-time sleeps
I hold a picture of your face
There watching, there winking
In the colour of my dreams

In the nearness of end
As the tide of night-time sleeps
I hold a picture of your face
Still staring, still smiling
In the fade watch of my dreams

In the nearness of end
As the tide of night-time sleeps
You curl in the drift of dry darkness
Shimmering the flight of light
You shadow the eve of my dreams

In the nearness of end
As the tide of night-time sleeps
You ghost in the float of pure present
You wash in the glow of grow
I sink in the hollow of my dreams

In the nearness of end
As the tide of night-time sleeps
A quiver, a flap of the familiar
Muzzy in the muffle of illusion
I'm landed in lost dreams

In the nearness of end
As the tide of night-time sleeps
I wake drenched in the wet of wave's loss
Shored in the forgotten, the abyss of pitched past
You sail outside my dreams…

Like a loud echo
Like a pungent scent
Like a soulless picture
It lived inside

I blocked my ears
Held my nose
Bit my pillow
Shielded my eyes
It lived inside

I ran to hide

I jumped on nails
Poisoned my body
Smothered my spirit
Drowned my soul
It lived inside

I lay still
Lifted my head
Heard my truth
Honoured its ache
She sighed inside

Afloat in warm darkness
Waves of memories, gladness
Treading waters of a sun-laced lake
At last inside, a welcome break

Alone without loneliness
Drenched in the cool kiss of calmness
No storms in this roomy tomb–
Tame tones, cushion colours, a vacuum

No wind to fight, no rocks to climb
sealed coated pain of time
Smooth-edged thoughts in which to loiter
Wallowing in a womb of water

Turning, bending, rolling, diving
In liquid velvet I'm surviving
At last a dome in which to retreat
At last a home in soul, a seat

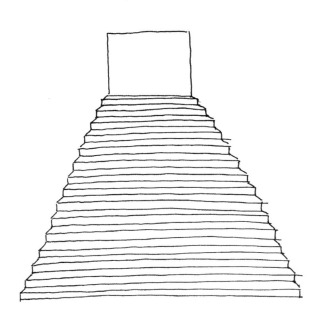

The Dawn

This walk is mine and mine alone
A winter day inside
As children jump and laugh around
I leave all that behind

It's raining now, I cannot see
A sun beyond the cloud
The shelter of your love for me
Lies shattered on the ground

Each step is near the end for me
No matter what you say
When you put on my brother's shoes
You'll know my rage today

Till then, I walk the plank of life
Preparing for a fall
Who sent me on this terror trip
Who dared to make that call

What did I do, what did I say!
Who robs my life from me!
If I could see your smirking eyes
I'd slap your face and scream.

But you're the one that greets me now
Wet casket on the pier
If you could share this hour with me
You'd know this room of tears

When seagulls skim an open sky
I stop to wonder who am I
The self I was, the self I lost
The self who survived at any cost

As she takes flight, bird of broken wings,
Broken bones,
Broken dreams,
Broken hope
She smiles for eternity
The smile of maybe,
The smile of wonder,
The smile of preparing song…

"Good bye," I say
"I hope we meet again"
"We will," "maybe" "who knows"
She chirps along
Checking the span of her wings
She blinks and stares afar

"I was never witty," she says, making me laugh
"But I was happy with John"
I nod and breathe to leave,
"Good bye is only a gesture" she flaps
And hobbling from her branch,
Tidying tubes, on the way
She lifts her wings for another day…

Do you need me when you're gone
Do you see my candle in the night
Do you stop to wonder why
What is my notion of the Sky?

Do you need me when you're gone
Do you eat, sleep or look on
Do you feel my shudder in your dying
What is my notion of the Sky?

You don't need me when you're gone
You don't see my candle in the night
You don't stop to wonder why
Is this my notion of the Sky?

You don't need me when you're gone!
You don't eat, sleep or ever look on!
You don't feel my violence in your dying!
This is my notion of the Sky!

I need you when you're gone!
I need your story to tell my mine
I need you confirming – verifying!
Is this my notion of the Sky?

I need you when you're gone
You need me to carry on
We wrote a book... a symphony... a song!
We carved a Hymn beyond the Sky...

Separated
Searching whole
Tripped in tease
Torched in darkness
Stood alone

Fallen to fear
Attached to hold
Delivered in ache
Soiled in doubt
I awake

Exposed
Crushed in loss
Surrendered to willing
Offered to heal
A new beginning

Guided to Self
Lead to Light
Transcended in breath
Bathed for love
I live

In blissful wait of feeling now
My heart is pounding, screaming Ow!
Newly born, black is white
Almost there, seeing light

The worst is over, my life begins
Another push, sailing sins
A sunny day, a storm in May
Whatever's there, is there today

It's been a while, years indoors
Opening boxes, doing chores
Returning frocks that didn't fit
Paying dearly for those that did

O look at me without my clothes
A laughing nude, I hope it shows!
Open arms, smiles apart
Feeling good, I like the start!

Once upon a time
I was you
Staying secret
Being true

What happened child
Of golden hair
What happened then
I wasn't there

Running wild
Laughing free
Bursting sun
You reached for me

But another won your heart
That day
A smiling lie
Danced your way

You followed him
Into a wood
No one saw
The wolf in hood

And now you stand
And stare at me
Your frock is stained
Your knees are green

How do I hold your hand and stay
How do I heal
That death
In May

This day
This night
This hour
Long due

This ink
This page
This prayer
For you…

And then my number was called
The dread of no name
The cubicle of alone
The chapter saying "dead"

Name, date of birth, she said
"Not me. Not now," I mimed, losing breath
Everything. Nothing
In the waiting room of death

What was the running from?
What was the running to?
Too late
In the waiting room of death

White floors
Consoling smiles
Buried
In the waiting room of death

What is this pull and drag for you
The golden road to fold
What is this steely ache I feel
In body mind and soul
I see you in a fallow field
I see you dance in wind
I see you in the nearest smile
I see you in the sinned
And there I drink you fill in bold
And swallowed thirst for more
What is this tug and steal for you
O! God please fill my more!

And then there is not knowing
When maps are maps
Knowledge is knowledge
Wisdom fails to inform
And the alone of that

When the flapping in darkness stops
When answers offer no meaning
When terror burns to silence
And the still shot of that

When being is all there is
When breath is love's experience
When expectations stop
And the godly hour of that

When giving is receiving
When running nowhere stops
When losing is beginning
And the grace of knowing that

Magic flutes sing mid-air
Smiles kiss our cheeks
Rain is sun laughing out loud!
Lost, Gods dance in wonder!
And the glorious glory of that!

You wandered on my path last night
A shape so sure and free
In all my thirst and longing breath
I hugged you to my being

For once the steel I wear so well
Stayed sleeping in my bed
As I allowed your sweet behold
Roll over me instead

As one we wrapped in memory melt
The tears that ache forgot
The blanket of our loss fell through,
The hope that I had not

Soaring rays of golden blaze
We danced the midnight hour
For now, for then, forever when
We spun a silk of song

And then the dawn that night forgave
Your footprints in the sand
The store of more inside my heart
That rage could never find…

As dawn announced its day in June
At once I saw
At once I knew
There is no me and wanton dreams
If there is you
And all that seems

We are the same
And none without
As I breathe in
You breathe out
I am your sun, your moon and star
You are my Wake in Ain Soph Aur*

*No ending / God

I hold the fire that flames in here
I hold the lake that spills my tears
I hold the light that torches my way
I hold the rock that roots my stay

I hold the ghost that shivers past
I hold the wind that hails my mast
I hold the rod that thumps my back
I hold the fear that knots my sack

I hold the piano that tinkles my tune
I hold the volcano that melts my moon
I hold all these and so much more
I hold all knowing behind my door…

I am
There is
In we
I kiss